Ordering Information:

Quantity sales. Special discounts are available on quantity
purchases by corporations, associations, and others.
For details, contact the publisher at the address above.

Printed in the United States of America. First Edition

ISBN 978-0-9861483-0-9

1. BUS047000BUSINESS & ECONOMICS / Negotiating

2. BUS019000BUSINESS & ECONOMICS /
Decision-Making & Problem Solving

3. BUS071000BUSINESS & ECONOMICS / Leadership

For more information, visit: www.frontierprojectpress.com

the
FRONTIER
PROJECT

THE
CARTOGRAPHY
OF
NEGOTIATION

BY SCOTT WAYNE

WITH JASON ALLEN ASHLOCK

CONTENTS

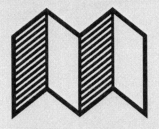

THE NEGOTIATOR'S MAP

INTRODUCTION

Negotiation is the art of creating value. By engaging parties that have some opposing and some mutual interests and bringing them into alignment, we capture and conjure value that would otherwise have evaporated.

As a society, we're rather dreadful at it.

We live in worlds of judgment and certainties, clinging to entrenched positions that give us shallow comfort in times of information overload and global chaos. News media declares "right" vs. "wrong". Social media reinforces that polarization. And our social graphs and media diets likely have us attending only to the voices that remind us that we're right.

In such an environment, we're losing our ability to see nuance, to empathise with another's position. And therefore we're losing our ability to collaborate and create value.[1] The more "certain" we become in our positions, the less we can see the other side. And if we can't see the other side, we'll be very weak negotiators indeed.

Negotiation is not about winning. It's about creating mutual value.

It's an irony we're not comfortable embracing: if you are to get what you really want, it's necessary to know what your target wants, too. And even to help them get it.

This book will teach you to fight that powerful cultural tide, to see multiple perspectives, and to create more value for yourself and those you work with, live with, compete with. Being a negotiator is a way of being, and a way of looking at the world: it's an ongoing search for better net outcomes as a result of two or more parties coming together to collaborate.

It's an endeavor that will bring you much satisfaction in life. This book is your invitation to a very noble pastime: to be a true negotiator.

[1] The U.S. Congress exemplifies this trend, though they're merely a highly visible expression of it. You could just as easily see it in private enterprises large and small, in schools, even in our families.

About Your Guide

Trained by the British Diplomatic Service. Studied International Relations and Security Studies at the London School of Economics and Georgetown University. Founded The Frontier Project, one of the fastest-growing private companies in America. Sought-after advisor and speaker to contemporary leaders. Leads discrete market investigations, brokers opportunities, and provides negotiation support for Fortune 100 companies, global non-profits, disruptive start-ups. Consults to boardrooms, negotiates in back rooms, speaks to ballrooms.

What This Isn't. What This Is.

There are some truly great books written on the theory of negotiation, and I offer my top reading recommendations at the end of this book. Richly researched and philosophically sound, they are foundational and essential—and numerous.

Theory is helpful. But sometimes you need more than abstraction. You need a guidebook for simply getting negotiation done. In my experience, there's plenty available to help you think about negotiation, but little good out there that tells you *how* to do it.

Hence this book: a brief guide to help you negotiate with customers and co-workers, clients and competitors, and even neighbors and family members. It's not designed to quote the research. You can find that someplace else. Instead, this is a handbook that describes the techniques and practices that will help you create new habits, eventually making you an instinctive, mutual-interest negotiator.

Small Punch-Packing Book

Size isn't everything. Most business books have one or two great concepts that could be covered in an article. But their publishers force their authors to fluff them out to big-book-size to sell as impressive things to put on one's office shelf (and to help the publishers swell their margins).

This book's size is proportionate to its content. It's meant to be small but mighty. And portable: I hope you will carry this around with you. Bend its spine. Re-read the passages that you need most. Scribble on its pages. Critique it. If you think it's shit, let us know. If it's transformative of your process, let us know that too.[2]

Tools

This book could have been like others in the category, including lots of diagrams with arrows and inverted triangles and a Venn or two. They would have sounded fancy and complicated, but you wouldn't use them. So instead

---

[2] Write us at hello@cartographyseries.com. Or use #CartographySeries on Twitter, LinkedIn, Facebook or Instagram.

we've created minimalistic tools that are more you than us. Simple prompts followed by open white spaces, similar to the back of a serviette,[3] where you scribble ideas late at night in a hotel bar.[4] Because given how busy you are, that's probably where you'll be doing your prep.

Sketching

These pages welcome ink from your pen or graphite from your pencil. But if you prefer to put your fingers to work moving electrons around your smartphone's screen, then doodle digitally by following the link or code provided beneath each blank page.

Why Cartography?

We in the West adore process. We like structure and step-by-step instructions. Business schools, in particular, encourage systems thinking and six-sigma-like approaches.

Negotiation doesn't work that way. There isn't a "negotiation process". And if you try to use one, any gifted negotiator will identify it, undermine it, and wreck your fixed process.

---

[3] That's a napkin, to those of you scribbling in an American hotel bar.

[4] The diagrams in this book are meant to be easily recreated on the back of a napkin—or on whatever scrap of paper is handy. Use them as frequently as necessary. For more on these tools and how we've used them, visit CartographySeries.com. And for additional exercises—and hands-on facilitation by experts—visit one of our Frontier Academy classes on Negotiation. You'll find more information on the last page of this book.

Each negotiation is different. Some techniques typically come before others. But we're dealing with complex issues and complex parties (i.e., highly emotional homo sapiens). Negotiations are iterative and circular. They jump around, abstractly connecting unexpected issues.

This book is written to reflect that. Read this book from beginning to end. Or don't: bounce around, if you like, from one topic to another.

Every great negotiator lays out a map for each particular negotiation, with the understanding that there are always more ways to journey toward a place than one can possibly predetermine. The work is analogous to that of a cartographer: You map out the issues, take note of the shifting landscape, and consider all the potential approaches to the final destination.

It's a science, but a highly interpretive one. Thus: The Cartography of Negotiation. Read the book as you'd read a map or a travel guide, not a business book or a novel. There are seven sections, but they don't represent seven truths or seven principles or seven lighthouses or seven mountains. They're merely containers for thought, insight, and preparation.

YOU

*The near absolute absence of personal reflection
time in our modern lives means many of us are
negotiating important issues with no idea of who
we truly are and what we truly want.*

YOU

It's All About You (At First)

Before you start negotiating anything, you need a starting point. That's you. This isn't as easy as it sounds.

You need to know who you are, what you want in life, and why.

An emerging hypothesis, explored by Timothy Wilson at the University of Virginia, proposes that we would rather experience pain than slow down and face ourselves. In Wilson's study, individuals inflicted electrical shocks on themselves to avoid sitting in a room alone with their thoughts for more than six minutes. Louis CK framed it so well that a video of his rant continues to rack up online views in the millions: we text and drive, putting ourselves in obvious danger, because we are frightened by the very idea of keeping company with only ourselves.[5]

We must work to reverse this trend in our mental engagement with ourselves. Without knowing ourselves, we cannot hope to have a base from which we effectively negotiate.

Negotiation is emotionally exhausting. Great negotiators know who they are, what drives them, what they want from life—and that knowledge is their grounding. It gives them the energy to negotiate with endurance and the strength to do it with focus.

Without grounding, you're just a hustler looking for random opportunities.

So let's start with: who are you? What's your manifesto for your life? The structure is simple; the mental work not as easy. Start with these statements.

[5] "Sometimes when things clear away and you're not watching anything and you're in your car... it starts to visit on you, just this sadness," he says. "And that's why we text and drive. People are willing to risk taking a life and ruining their own because they don't want to be alone for a second."

LIFE MISSION

I am…

A mother of two kids

A teacher

An entrepreneur

My higher calling is…

To teach others

To protect the environment

To be a great parent

My legacy will be…

Raising healthy children

Building a high performing business

A great book

✎ LIFE MISSION

I am…

My higher calling is…

My legacy will be…

Orbit of Matter

Next, let's work out who is important to you by building your personal solar system. I.e. Who it is you're working so hard to impress and provide for.

1. Write your name in the center of the page (you're the sun).

2. Now write the names of people in your orbit whom you care about (your planets). The closer they are to your sun, the more you care for them, and the more they matter.

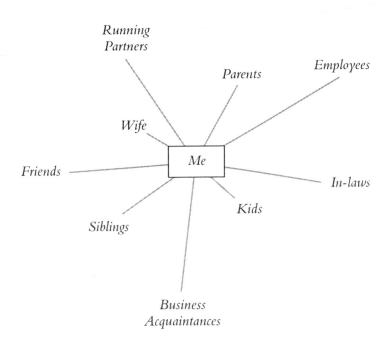

bit.ly/LetsSketch

Now let's filter that a little. Imagine you're told you have only six weeks to live.

Return to your orbit. Draw a dotted line around those with whom you would choose to spend your dying days.

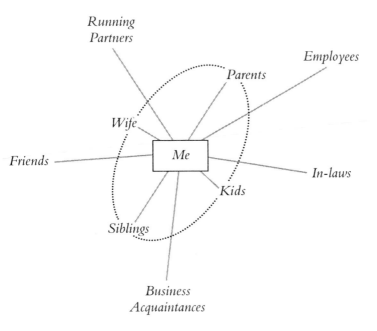

These are the people who truly matter to you. They are the people you're ultimately negotiating for. And these are the only people whose judgment you consider and whose opinion you internalize.

When you're exhausted, and considering giving up on finding a resolution, this is the page you stare at to remind yourself who you're negotiating *for*.

Life Design

So we have your life mission and we know the people who matter most to you. Now we identify what you want and what you need to fulfill the life you just sketched.

We create a Life Design.

You can sketch this in a notebook or create a spreadsheet or scribble on a napkin. Form doesn't matter. What does matter is that you're bluntly truthful about yourself to yourself.

In the left column, write a category. It could be income, or travel, or job, or spouse. In the three columns to the right, describe what you would be content with in that category, what would be good, and what would be great.

For example, in the category of job, you might be content with any job that paid over $50,000 per year. A job that allowed you to use your photography skills would be good. A job that allowed you to do both of these and travel internationally would be awesome.

	Okay	*Good*	*Great*
Income	*$50,000*	*$65,000*	*$80,000*
Job	*Desk Job*	*Desk Job & Travel*	*Desk Job & Travel & Influencer*
Travel	*Two Weeks*	*Four Weeks*	*Six Weeks*
Love	*Marriage*	*Marriage & Two Kids*	*Marriage & Five Kids*

Be precise about what you want and why. It's a good de-cluttering exercise—and you might discover there's a lot you assumed you need and want that you actually don't. The less you need, the stronger a negotiator you become.

	Okay	*Good*	*Great*

bit.ly/LetsSketch

	Okay	Good	Great

So now you know who you are and what you want. Everything you negotiate should be tied to serving your Life Mission, your Orbit of Matter or your Life Design. These are your *negotiating core*.

If the issue at hand isn't related to your core, you probably don't need or want it.

By tying everything you negotiate for to these three things, you ensure you have the passion, motivation and focus to negotiate hard. Without knowing this, you'll flounder in the face of a strong counterpart who is grounded in who they are.

For example, there's a difference between telling oneself "I'm going to negotiate a promotion" and telling oneself, "I'm going to negotiate a promotion and use the extra income to pay for online graduate school classes so that I'm qualified for a change in career to something I love".

Tying to something in your life design or your life mission statement gives you competitive focus and staying power.[6]

---

[6] For more on staying power, visit the Negotiators Diet in the Appendix.

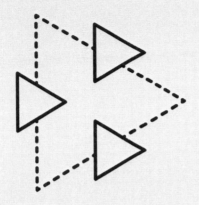

THEM

Now, get the hell out of your head and deep into theirs.

Oh, get into their heart too.

CHAPTER NO. 2

THEM

Signal-to-Noise Ratio

So you know what you want. Now you need to influence those that can provide it to you. To do that, you need to climb outside of your head and into theirs.

But first: a word on resonance. The relationship between content that will impact your target ("signal") and the total volume of chatter ("noise").

Great negotiators have very high signal-to-noise ratios. They don't say a lot. And when they speak, the content resonates powerfully and deeply with the target. Just like working on one's breathing pattern is a good practice for meditation, or working on one's stretching is great practice for an athlete, working on signal-to-noise ratio is good practice for a negotiator.

What Moves Your Target?

To get that signal-to-noise ratio right, we have to be able to think and feel like the target.

We start with basic data gathering. The sources for this research are innumerable, but you can start with the obvious: LinkedIn, Instagram, Facebook, Twitter, Pinterest, corporate websites, press articles, blogs.

A map of information from these sources can give you a deep picture of life by translating multiple points of data.

A cursory review of social media and press would generate this target map on me.

Higher Education
- London School of Economics and Political Science (BSC)
- Georgetown University (MA)

Family Man
- From Northern England
- Married
- Lives in Richmond with Family (Ryann and three kids)
- Enjoys running, traveling, hiking
- Business casual

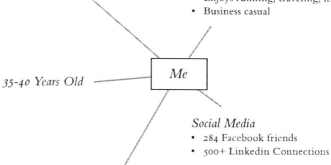

35-40 Years Old

Me

Social Media
- 284 Facebook friends
- 500+ Linkedin Connections

Politically Engaged, Extensive Business Background
- Previously worked in global finance, international affairs, business development; served on boards of global non-profits

Target Life Map: (Your Target)

bit.ly/LetsSketch

Target Life Mapping

You can further complete the target map by drawing on human sources of information—friends, colleagues, and personal assistants.

Beware, no one point of information can give you a deep understanding of a target, but overlapping, reinforcing points can generate a fairly reliable picture of the person you're targeting.

For example, being of the Roman Catholic faith doesn't confirm a great deal about the character and outlook of a person.

But being Roman Catholic, on the board of a Catholic Relief Services Charity, a member of the local school PTA board, and a "liking" pro-life organisations on social media organisations does give you a high degree of confidence in the target's outlook.

Likewise, a target "liking" the Sierra Club on Facebook tell us very little about the outlook of a target. But that "like", combined with photos wearing Patagonia clothing, retweets of Al Gore and driving a hybrid vehicle: that probably does.

Dirt Digging vs. Research

How much research is invasive and how much isn't? It's a hard line to draw.

Ask yourself: If my target discovers that I'm researching this they will be…

a) *Deeply complimented that I'm investing so much resource in understanding their perspective.*

b) *Thoroughly offended that I'm digging into their private life.*

Obviously, you'd like the answer to be A. Not B.

Someone might be life-mapping you right now.

Someone might be life-mapping you right now. Be flattered. It could be a good thing.

Or not.

If you've not taken care to properly represent yourself on the Internet, then the approaches you'll field and the inquiries that reach you are less likely to be of value. If you want to attract opportunities in line with your interests and ambitions, make sure the thoughtful people—like yourself, and others reading this book—can find you and know you.

Each case will be slightly different. For me, if you're calling my assistant to find my preference in time to meet, that's great.[7] If you're calling to find out if I have a good relationship with my parents, I'll probably be offended.

Hopes & Fears

Consider the life map of your target. Now engage in an imaginative act: What, if you were them, would you be hopeful of? Afraid of? Note: this is not if you were in their role, but if you were actually them—with their personality, their life situation and their role.

---

[7] For reference, I much prefer to have afternoon meetings rather than mornings. For me, mornings are prime creative real estate, and I protect them for my own work. Find your own rhythm, then send invitations and set meeting times accordingly.

HOPES	FEARS
Moving to California	*Losing job*
Promotion to director level	*Not being geographically close to family*
Vacationing to Asia	
Getting a dog	*Not learning anything new, stuck in a rut*

This is now your template for understanding. Everything you offer and every way in which you speak will serve one of these purposes: helping your target reach their hopes or reduce the risk of their fears becoming reality.

If you manage this, your signal-to-noise ratio will be exceptionally high. Because everything you say will resonate with your target's hopes or fears. They'll feel like you truly know them and what moves them. They'll feel that you respect them. Because...well...you do.

This is a big investment of time, but it will pay off multiple-fold.

Logic is Overrated

Despite what we often assume, business decisions are rarely based on logic. They're based on emotion, ego, identity, and physiology. Okay, and a tiny bit of logic. Like this:

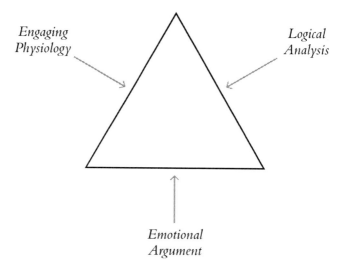

Engaging Physiology

Logical Analysis

Emotional Argument

This is the influence triangle. If you want to influence somebody, you have to hit them from all three angles: logical analysis, emotional argument, engaging physiology. Obsess about all sides of the triangle as you make your case. But know that in order of importance, emotion and physiology beat the pants off logic.

Forget your Sales Training

Selling is about need-creation and need-fulfillment. Negotiation is about rearranging assets to solve the needs of different groups to mutual benefit.

If we're better salespeople, more stuff will get sold. If we're better negotiators, more value will be created.

Selling is premised on providing solutions to (perceived) needs in return for cash. Negotiation, done correctly, is premised on mutual empathy and collaborative creativity to solve problems. Often selling relies on a pre-existing product set; success is determined by how frequently and for how much money one can match that product set to a need, whether real or imagined. Negotiation, on the other hand, creates a new product—and only after mining the interests of both parties.

Good salespeople generate a lot of sales. Good negotiators generate a lot of value.

Similar, but different.

Deploying sales techniques in negotiations can create dissonance and distrust. Tread carefully.

(Though some of the very best "salespeople" are actually great value-creating negotiators, forced by their employers to have "sales" on their business cards.)

bit.ly/LetsSketch

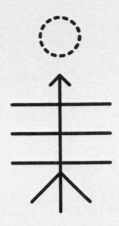

ACCESS

In a time-starved world, gaining access to the
right target is an enormous part of any negotiation.

ACCESS

Gaining Access

So you know your target, and you have a good sense of what drives them. Now we need to gain access to them.

If they're senior and/or powerful, direct access may be hard, so start by mapping people who have direct access to your target. This can include their co-workers, friends, and family.

Overleaf, you'll find an access map for me. It's far easier to get a message through some of these points, than it is to get a meeting with me directly. The transaction often makes more sense too.

Do you want:

a) *Ten minutes with the executive?*
b) *An hour with a trusted advisor to the executive?*

It's likely that you'll have more chance at expressing your case in option B, and that you'll have the opportunity to be "recommended" to the top executive by that person. A phrase we often hear from our top executive clients is "Should I listen/trust this person?" Therefore, an endorsement from a trusted advisor can mean a lot. Our egos want option A, our smart minds should seek option B.

🔍	*Look up Scott on Linkedin to get information*
✉	*Email assistant, Andrew, requesting a thirty minute pitch*
✓	*Request accepted*
🕐	*Thirty minute meeting with Andrew*
✉	*Request second meeting with Scott*
👍	*Andrew recommends you*
🏴	*Meet with Scott*

Access Map: Your Target

1. *Draw your map.*
2. *Trawl your contacts (LinkedIn can help here), and map anyone who can connect you to the map.*
3. *Cash in favours. Seek an introduction—with your access pitch included.*

The Access Pitch

This is your punchy, short message, and it's always about them. Its length and detail need only be sufficient enough for them to agree to an official meeting. So make it memorable. And keep it short.

Someone on your access map may indeed be positioned to help you gain the access you seek—but only if you enable them to help you with as little effort as possible. The key to this stage is not pitching a solution, but hitting a resonant note of interest that gets you the meeting during which the first round of discussion takes place.

Here are a couple of examples:

Access Pitch Examples

1. As I understand it...

   You're seeking to win the annual business growth awards...
   I believe plugging in our sales distribution system may
   enhance your product sales.
   May I arrange a 30-minute meeting through your PA?

2. As I understand it...

   You're seeking to work fewer hours in the current role.
   I believe there's a different staffing model that might
   be able to deliver that flexibility.
   May I set up a time to talk for 30 minutes about this
   with your PA?

Notice that with the access pitch, all the language is about them. Their hopes. Their fears. You'll get to what you want in the formal meeting. Your access pitch is merely making it easy for them to agree to a brief meet.

The use of the phrase "I believe" shows some humility. It doesn't imply the same level of "rightness" as it would if you were to say "I know". You may be wrong: Opening up that possibility ensures that you don't appear to know better than they do. Thus lessening the chance they'll disregard your approach immediately

It's structured to make it effortless for them to agree to a meeting. They know it will be short (30 mins). They know what's up for discussion. They know what they might take from it. And they don't even have to check their calendar—you're going to work with their assistant. All they have to do is reply with a "yes" and you do the rest.

Then you pick up the call to the assistant, and with full, honest, friendly integrity say "Hey, Samantha has just emailed agreeing to meet in the next few weeks. Do you have a few minutes to check availability?" If yes: "When are good times for Samantha and what location does she prefer?"

You then follow up with a thank-you email or hand-written note[8] to the assistant. They're going to be critical to moving this forward.

---

[8] Notes through the mail are seen as "gifts"; email is simply "work".

Executive Assistants

Frequently ignored, regularly taken for granted, often patronised.

Treat with respect and dignity. Assume to be very smart. Don't try to charm or befriend. These are insanely smart people who run the worlds of insanely powerful people. They are trusted and trustworthy. They have insight and wisdom. Politely seek their professional advice and counsel and opinions. They're enormous reservoirs of information and managers of influence. But never forget that their ultimate loyalty remains to those they serve. If your interests are aligned with those of their employer, you will fair well. If not, you won't. Influence in good, transparent faith.

bit.ly/LetsSketch

INTERESTS

Screw your position. Park your judgment of others.

What's your interest?

INTERESTS

Let's say I believe drug use and prostitution should be legalised. You may believe they should be outlawed. These are our positions—firmly held, honourably believed, passionately defended. Both positions potentially right, both potentially wrong. If we negotiate from such positions, we'll enjoy the fleeting rush of self-righteousness, but it's not very likely that we'll get anywhere in seeking a path forward that progresses better community.

But if we negotiate from common *interests*—"protecting the safety and rights of women" perhaps, or "reducing harmful drug use"—we can collaborate on a whole range of issues related to the problems we wish to solve and the progress we wish to see. We make incremental but impactful changes to the issues without necessarily giving up on our overarching values.

Defending a personal position can sabotage any negotiation: you can't move forward when you're channeling all your energy to standing your ground. But you can move forward when you're focused on where we agree, rather than disagree, and build from that base.

We don't need to agree with the values of the other party in order to make progress. We don't even need to respect one another. We just need to have some degree of overlapping interests. It's in that shared space that constructive outcomes can be negotiated.

Don't try to align your differing positions. In most cases, it won't be possible. Instead, frame the negotiation around your mutual interests.

Negotiators focus on interests. Ideologues and idiots focus on positions.

Should the NRA and liberal groups talk about gun control or gun rights? Absolutely not. Should they share ideas on the safety of children in schools? Absolutely yes. Neither group has shared positions, but both groups have shared interests: namely, children in safe learning environments.

Should the union talk to the management about job cuts or job guarantees? Probably not. Should they share ideas on creating a growth company in the mid-term? Absolutely yes. The two don't share positions, but they do share interests: stability and profitability of an organization with obligations to employees.

Your Turn. What should your two parties not be talking about? What should they be?

When Shouldn't You Negotiate?

When do you tell them to go to hell? Never. But you do walk away sometimes.

If the other party's goal is your destruction or harm—physical, political, economic—there's no rationale in negotiating. This explains Israel's position on Iran (absolutely no negotiating[9]) versus Egypt (constant, constructive discussions). Iran desires the destruction of Israel. Egypt does not. Therefore, with the latter, there's room for mutually better outcomes through negotiation rather than conflict.

There are very few of these situations. In the antagonistic heat of a negotiation, it's very easy to see your foe as an existential threat. They very probably are no such thing.

They might be worthy of a battle, however. And it is very possible to fight and negotiate at the same time. During the Northern Irish "Troubles", the British Government and the Irish Republican Army were in regular negotiations while in the midst of direct conflict. The IRA did not seek the destruction of the British state; it sought an end to British control of Northern Ireland. And the British Government did not seek the destruction of the people of the IRA or Sein Fein, but their cessation of certain activities. Thus there was room for negotiation, which ultimately proved fruitful, if delicate.

[9] This is their position. It's likely that they're back-channel negotiating in some form or other on specific issues.

This applies in corporate life too. One can aggressively compete with a colleague for a promotion or an international assignment, while simultaneously negotiating with them on fair process or splitting the outcome.

Negotiation is Innovation

Once we've identified our shared interests...

We need to reduce costs to save the company.

We want to improve the education of our city's kids.

We want to end the conflict.

...Only then can we move the negotiation to collaborative ideation.

Here are the rules. There are only two.

1. *All ideas are welcome. Even those that might be politically incorrect or sensitive.*
2. *We don't critique ideas; we build on them.*

The point of this stage is simply to expand our thinking and extend the list of possible options. You want as much as possible on the table. You'll sort through it later. But the more ideas and opportunities you have now, the more options you have to build agreement. And at this stage, options are of highest value.

The simplest ideation tool is a blank sheet with a hundred blank spaces. As a combined negotiation team—your team and your "rivals"—you generate as close to one hundred potential solutions to the issues as possible. No matter how impossible or ludicrous, they make the list. This phase allows for venting the ridiculous and radical, the bold and the muted. And creates options on the negotiating table that we'd never thought of earlier—and the more options, the more "lubricant" for reaching agreement.

Single Issue v Multiple Issue Negotiations

The ever-present risk in any negotiation is that the parties become bogged down in emotional mud, each side slugging away with the same tired artillery, having nothing in the armory to move the engagement along.

In many such cases, the negotiations have become stuck because the parties have decided to isolate a single issue on which to engage. Often this is "price". Or a belief: "gun rights" vs "gun control". When there's only a single issue on the table, it's easy to become bogged down in positions and lose sight of our interests.

The solution to this is to actively transform single-issue negotiations into multi-issue negotiations, thereby providing us with more options to make small movements in different areas. Ideally, you are able to blend issues that fall on the spectrum of openness and difficulty.

Alpha v Beta

Two airlines—Alpha Airways and Beta Airlines—are negotiating a merger.

Alpha Airways places strategic value on a single fleet brand (Boeing), keeping its name, and holding on to its award winning website. Beta Airlines does not view these issues as strategic imperatives.

For Beta, headquarter location, engine preference (Rolls Royce), and international network partners are highly valued, while significantly less important to Alpha.

Both airlines place extreme value on their ticketing software platforms, aircrew seniority systems, and union agreements. Neither cares significantly about their call centers, catering providers, or advertising agency relationships.

To keep open negotiations on issues that both parties care about, the parties should regularly take a break from discussing those core issues in order to lubricate movement with a blend of trading high-to-low value issues, passing back and forth the small issues that neither feel strongly about. One key to reaching agreement is keeping momentum around the value of the bigger picture by creating a strong enough rhythm of success that both parties want to remain at the table. A big outcome should be reinforced by a runway to the big agreement, created by a series of small wins by each side.[10]

Whenever you're confronted with a single-issue negotiation, do all you can to add a blend of additional tradable issues to the conversation.

This trading back and forth of issues—one side gaining what they value, the other side giving up what they don't—provides goodwill, relieves turbulence, and creates momentum on the issues that both parties value greatly.

Priming. Anchoring. Framing.

At this stage, let's break to introduce three key concepts you'll see negotiators deploying. When a novice, simply be aware of them. As an advanced practioner, begin to actively deploy in negotiations.

---

[10] With the implicit threat that the series of valuable small wins will all be lost if the bigger prize is not agreed upon.

PRIMING

When I tell you what to see, you'll see it. When I tell you what you'll feel like, you're more likely to feel that way.

Let's take a medical example. In our work in healthcare, we'll coach physicians and nurses to actively prime patients to look for positive attributes. There's an enormous difference in patient perceptions of their doctor when a nurse or administrator chooses to say:

"Dr Gupta is your attending physician today. She's tremendous. Great person and terrific physician."

Rather than:

"Dr Gupta is your attending physician today. She'll likely be a while as she has a huge workload today."

Time and time again, we see patient satisfaction survey scores rise as a result of simple priming cues like this. The concept is simple: if we prime you to tell you the doctor is terrific, you'll look for evidence of that. When we prime you that the doctor is overloaded with work, you'll look fore evidence that she's distracted and not listening to you.

Sadly, with simple cues like this we can create great patient scores for doctors, regardless of their clinical effectiveness—but it speaks to the power of priming.

You can try this with colleagues. If you're negotiating a deal in which your team are part of the product, you can actively prime. Let's imagine we're in early rounds of negotiations for my firm to work with you.

Over coffee, I tell you that you simply must meet my media producer, because she's brilliant and driven, able to produce whatever multimedia asset you're hoping for. When you and the producer eventually meet for a coffee of your own, you're immediately looking for evidence of that competence, and you'll be very likely to find it, quickly reinforcing your view of the firm's capabilities.

Or:

Over coffee I mention you might want to meet with my media producer. I don't say anything more, but I raise one eyebrow and shrug slightly. When you meet with that producer, if you ever do, you're looking for evidence of my skepticism or dismissal. And you'll be very likely to find it.

In the lead up to a negotiation, if we reiterate how complex the negotiation is likely to be, then the other party is likely to prepare for lengthy, drawn-out discussions. If we prime in early correspondence that we feel this is a relatively light transaction relative to our previous deals, the other party are more likely to prepare for a rapid discussion and agreement.

Priming is so common an act we tend to overlook its power. Reclaim it. Set expectations in the lead-up to the negotiation event by using the language of fairness and mutuality. Back this up with word choice, tone of voice and facial expression.

ANCHORING

All information is relative. All decision-making is done in a comparative dynamic. For us to place value on something, we need an "anchor" against which we measure it. Something's always better or worse than something else. Anchoring is determining what the something else is— ideally ahead of the negotiation of value.

To illustrate, try answering this question:

Is a train traveling at an average speed of 90 miles per hour a fast train?

However you answered that question, you consciously or subconsciously anchored speed as being relative to something else. But with this type of question, there isn't a correct answer. We need an anchor.

Is a train traveling at an average speed of 90 miles per hour on a French SNCF high-speed rail line between Paris and Lille a fast train?

Is a train traveling at 90 miles per hour on the American Amtrak route between Washington DC and New York a fast train?

In the case of the first question, with the anchor being our knowledge of French high-speed rail capabilities, the answer is likely "no". In the latter question, with our knowledge of the rickety Amtrak system and the snarled traffic on Interstate 95, our answer is more likely "yes". In each question, the train is traveling at the same average speed. What shifts is the anchor.

In any negotiation it's ideal that you shape the anchors—the relative measure of value. At a minimum, you must be agreeing the anchors in cooperation with the other party. Never allow the anchor to be fully determined by the other side. The valuation of a business relative to its five-year or ten-year performance can generate dramatically different ballparks of price negotiation. Negotiating your salary increase relative to peers in your company or peers in your industry can have equally dramatic variations. Manage the anchors.

Borrowing from Mickey Mouse

You've been to the theme park—Disneyland and the like—where you're standing in an enormous queue for a five-minute ride. The signage on the line tells you that the average wait time is 45 minutes. You sigh at the idea of standing in the baking sun that long, but your seven year old desperately wants to have a turn on the ride. You resign yourself to a long wait. But 30 minutes later, you find yourself at the front of the line. Pleasantly surprised that the wait was "fifteen minutes faster" than "normal".

Does this mean the queueing science of the theme park has gone awry on this one day? Not at all. Their experience engineers are overriding their logistics people to overstate the queue time in order to shift the focus of guests from "We had to wait 30 minutes for the ride!" to "The queue was 15 minutes faster than we expected!" Without the signage, anything over 10 minutes is a long wait. With the 45 minutes sign "anchoring" our expectation, 30 minutes is relatively fast.

You can apply this approach to the negotiation process itself. Consider the example above regarding priming the other party regarding a negotiation's length. If you're hosting the negotiation, you might over-estimate the length of time the discussions are likely to take. That way, when you close the agreement early, you're "gifting" back time to the participants.

> They feel a reduction in stress as they now have additional time to catch up with other responsibilities. They'll leave the discussions with an extra reason to be upbeat, increasing the likelihood they'll be open to future deals with you.

FRAMING

"The negotiators are negotiating about the negotiations". A seemingly nonsensical phrase you'll hear in news media from time to time. Whether it be an American team negotiating about whether to negotiate with the Iranians, or business rivals determining whether they might discuss a merger, these discussions are critical and often better run through backchannels rather than through formal discussion.[11]

So let's untangle that phrase. What the advance team are negotiating over is the "frame" of the formal negotiations: i.e., what will be on, and off, the table for discussion. Without agreement of the frame, the discussions shouldn't move forward.

---

[11] A note about backchannels. Governments call this track II diplomacy: the informal, unofficial communications handled by proxies rather than primary parties. There are times when such intermediaries are valuable, especially in a cross-cultural situation or when the optics of a party speaking with you outside of a formal setting might endanger the viability of an effective negotiation session later.

A young analyst has planned a vacation and suddenly there's a major deal in the works that threatens to keep her at her desk. When she plans her weekly check-in with her manager, she will remember their lunch from the month before, during which he reminded her to seek a balance of work and personal time. To have the conversation she wants to have, she'll use words she can win with: "balance" and "family" and "recharge". She'll avoid words that will distract: "Brazil" and "beach" and "no wifi". While the details of her trip will emerge, if she's set the frame of the discussion around the values she shares with her manager, those details will not set the terms of the discussion; rather, they'll be understood in relation to the established frame.

Determining what's outside the frame is just as import-ant as determining what's within it. Proactively frame your negotiations and remain very aware of being framed by the other party.

To understand framing, imagine that you're staring at a piece of art in a museum. You know where to look because the artist has placed the art in a frame to tell you that it's "art". Anything outside the frame is background.

The same concept applies to negotiations. What's inside the frame and what's outside the frame can have dramatic implication for outcome. Ideally you should be actively framing, but at a minimum you should be acutely aware of what's in and out of frame before you start formal negotiations.

One can frame a discussion formally or informally. In the formal sense it might be along the lines of: "The parties agree to discuss collaboration in overseas markets, but the domestic market is off the table". Or informally, through word selection that ties to the other party's hopes and fears. Keep anything that will derail or distract, outside of frame.

Imagine If....

Imagine if we in the United States didn't talk of positions like "Gun Control" or "Gun Rights", but of mutual interests in "Ensuring Schools are Safe for Kids". Would we still be in the grip of deadlock, even after so many massacres? Or would we being to see collaborative brainstorming between the pro-gun and anti-gun movements. Their positions are incongruous. But their interests in this one arena are entirely aligned.

Maybe we'd see PTSD-exposed military veterans in schools, acting alongside armed security officers, with the informed ability to recognise mental health issues. While there, they might encourage students to serve in the armed services, Peace Corps, Teach for America. Funding: a small sales tax on bullets, sponsored by the NRA.

Who doesn't want to see veterans mentoring youth, American military recruiting for the country's best service-oriented organizations, the armed services properly manned, schools flooded with volunteers, and students later representing their country overseas, and of course schools given protection in keeping with the treasure they contain?

Filtering Options

Once you have the reservoir of ideas, we can start to filter what's valuable and viable. Critical at this stage is asking, "Is this possible"? instead of "Is this the easiest"? Resist the temptation to rank ideas or show obvious preference. Strike only the options that are impossible, not the ones that are unlikely. Your job is to keep the "possibles" on the list as long as you can.

If you can keep pushing the possible, you'll reinforce your framing: that the negotiation is defined by shared interests. Giving you—and the other party—a chance to create greater value for you both.

Pathways

To effectively push the extremes of what's possible, we have to do some convincing. We do that by demonstrating the credible pathways that might lead to the possibilities we've managed to keep on the list.

Pathbuilding is critical to persuasion. As you sift through the various versions of what's possible, swiftly provide supporting ideas as to what path might get you there. If you know ahead of time (and you should know ahead of time—see the sidebar) some of the outcomes that you think you can pull off, be sure that you've thought of a credible pathway to get there before you get in the room.

In the heat of negotiation, parties will lean toward the credible. And as the parties fatigue, the laid out and comprehensible path will be the one they head toward. Humans love movement and define experience in terms of progress. A path indicates both. Whether or not you love the destination is secondary to whether or not you feel like you're moving toward an end.[12]

---

[12] Theologians call this teleology. Chess masters term it the end game. A certain breed of deconstructionist philosophers might label it the death wish. A parent on a road trip will identify it as a child's backseat refrain: are we there yet? Whatever you call it, the urge is the same: to know we're headed toward conclusion.

The Globe Theatre vs. Second City

When next in London, visit the Globe, the historic site of the some of the earliest staged performances of Shakespeare's timeless comedies and dramas. Buy a ticket to whichever of his plays is on offer, and watch the masters of the Royal Shakespeare Company enliven a script passed down across centuries.

When next in Chicago, visit Second City, the iconic institution devoted to the craft of improvisational comedy. Buy a ticket to whatever experience they're crafting while you're in town, and watch the artists on stage marshal their creative spontaneity to produce a one-of-a-kind, non-repeatable experience.

Negotiation is less like The Globe and more like Second City. There are confines in which you play, but there is no script. You can prepare and rehearse, but your time on the stage will require you to bob and weave amongst countless variables. You can know generally where you're headed with your fellow performers, but the process will be written right in front of you.

And you can prepare, but you cannot predetermine. Before you begin, you should know very well a few of the outcomes you hope to achieve, and have in mind the pathways that could get you there. But you and the other parties aren't working off the same script. Be willing to go off-book. There might very well be a better version of the story to be found along the way.

bit.ly/LetsSketch

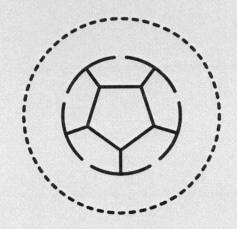

ENVIRONMENT

The President negotiates at Camp David for a reason.

ENVIRONMENT

The Negotiation Venue

Their office is a very bad idea. Their conference room is slightly better. Better options: a quiet coffee shop, a hotel conference room, an arrivals lounge at an airport or train terminal, going for a walk. Neutral territory is good. If it's a tense issue, neutral territory is critical.

Look for spaces that allow room to breathe. Camp David, Chequers, and other Presidential and Prime Ministerial retreats exist for a reason. They're detached from the institution. They're separated from symbols and sounds of other influencers. They're variations of the typical environment, with modularity included: outside or inside, formal or casual, spacious or intimate.

If you can get your target to a different space, they'll be primed to think differently.

Invitations

They'll want to meet on their territory. Just as you would.

To get them to that different space, offer a place that's convenient to them by reason of their lifestyle or schedule. Suggest a coffee shop in an airport where they'll be on layover. A restaurant near where they pick up their kids. A café near their place of worship. A conference room in the building of a mutual partner.

Ideal: a meeting spot that poses no disruption to day or style, perhaps adds interest, and creates neutral space.

Cool Hands

Before you go into the meeting, go to the bathroom. Wash your hands in cold water and dry thoroughly with a paper towel. Don't use a hand dryer if you can help it.

Handshakes affect first impressions. Cool, dry hands signal control and authority. Warm, sweaty hands…well, they represent warm, sweaty hands.

True Colours

There's a whole pile of science, and another pile of myths, around the colours one should wear in a negotiation.

Don't take it too seriously. But, in the West at least, stay away from:

RED	Signals caution, danger
GREEN	Suggests liberal, environmental
BLACK	Symbolizes aggression, death

And lean toward:

BLUE	Calming
PURPLE	Neutrality
WHITE	Honest

Try them. (Not a white suit with a purple shirt though.)

Take this list with you.
Visit bit.ly/True_Colours to download and share.

Where You Sit Determines Where You Stand

Sitting across a table from one another, talking eyeball to eyeball, encourages a sense of confrontation. You're literally looking at the world from opposite directions. Your eyes, and theirs, create a directional line—sitting across from one another suggests you may be about to collide.

Ideal: Your feet directly intersecting theirs at 90 degrees. In this arrangement, you can make and break eye contact comfortably and informally.

Or perhaps, don't sit at all.

If you need to have a difficult conversation, try walking it off. You'll be side by side, a representation of alliance. And you're moving forward together—implying a mutually agreed-upon destination. And there will be plenty of distractions to break the intensity. If you need to talk the tough stuff, do it while moving.

To cover a lot of tense ground in a short amount of time, with far less intensity than sitting across a conference room table, try these twelve words: "Shall we walk a few blocks and grab a cup of coffee?"

Project, Don't PowerPoint

Negotiators negotiate. Entertainers perform. If you want to demote yourself from negotiator to entertainer, switch on PowerPoint.

The moment you throw a slide upon a screen, meeting participants lean back to watch, putting them in a posture of "entertain me". In an instant, you have made yourself submissive to the other party. The implications of this are significant enough to derail any chance of a successful negotiation just as you've begun. Your tone and rate of speech, logical approach, hand gestures, eye contact, and entire group dynamics are transformed when you are shifted from conversationalist to presenter.

Don't do it. Ever. No matter how pretty your deck. No matter how perfect your visuals. And no matter how much more comfortable you might feel reading from a prepared collection of slides. Kick out this crutch and you'll travel much further.

If you need graphics, data or other illustrations to support your case, then print those assets on cards or paper. Pass them between the participants in the meeting. Have your targets lean in to study your material, not lean back to be entertained by your case.

Focus on projecting your argument, not your slides.

Secret Signals

Repeat after me. "We will not arrange secret signals as a negotiation team."

Any decent negotiator will spot your team's secret signals early in the proceedings. If they're sophisticated, they'll then start replicating those signals knowing that you may mirror them and incorrectly signal to your team.

It also makes you look dumb and insecure.

If you want to tug at your earlobe during talks, tug at your earlobe... Just don't have it mean anything other than your ear is itchy.

Number 2 is Number 1

Consider having your number 2 most senior person on the team do most of the talking—and sit in the centre of the team. This sets your senior negotiator free to observe and interpret the other side, and enables them to step in and discreetly rescue if things go awry.

Roles

However large or small your team, agree ahead of time on roles. When a team can ably and comfortably look to one another for key information or support, you'll all appear confident and prepared. Any hint of competition among your team will be sniffed out and leveraged against you. All team sports define positions. Get yours straight well ahead of time. (See the final section of the book for more on the importance of rehearsal.)

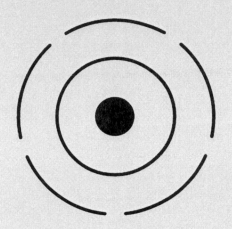

PRESENCE

The greatest impediment to being a great negotiator?
It's in your pocket.

Switch off the phone. Get in the zone.

PRESENCE

In the Zone

The first impressions you make on a target are critical. Ahead of the meeting, here's what you won't be doing:

Staring at your smart phone.

Here's what you will be doing:

Nothing.
Sit. Stand. Steadily. With open face and alert eyes.
Be Present.

When you're distracted by a smart phone, the target's first impression of you is the top of your head as you stare downwards. Or the grimace of judgment on your face as you contemplate the email that you're reading. Or that especially unimpressive slouching posture that our bodies naturally achieve when our smart phone captivates us.

It exudes great confidence to sit quietly with composure. When you're sitting straight, they see your eyes. They see you are calm. They see you are prepared. They see you are present.

Lobbies & Receptions

Once you're on-site, do not talk about the negotiation. If the other party is running a tight operation, then anything you say might be overhead and fed back to them. Extend this restraint to nearby coffee shops and sidewalks. This isn't paranoia. It's good sense.

(Trust me: If you make comments in the waiting area of our Studio ahead of a pitch to us, our receptionist will be live-streaming that commentary by instant message to our team. It's fair game intelligence in public space.)

Hotels

Take care not to stay at the same hotel as the other party. You'll not only reduce the risk of any of your planning being overhead, but you'll also give your team a break from the negotiating environment after hours. This is important for mental stamina and *esprit d'corps*. Stay somewhere else.

And it's slightly awkward bumping into your counterparts in your gym gear.

Mise en Place

A negotiation lesson worth learning from the other CIA: the Culinary Institute of America: Have everything in place before the event.

The French culinary concept of *mise en place*—roughly "everything in place"—speaks to the thoughtful preparation of resources and materials and accouterment ahead of the dinner, and its appropriate placement during the event. Done right, the chef is able focus on the precision necessary to create the prefect dish, rather than concerning himself with the details of supplies and ingredients.

It applies equally to negotiation.

Become practised in having your tools in the same place at all times. Here's a check list of what should be in your briefcase, stored in the same location, and carried with you at all times.

☐ *Two pens. One for the other party should they forget). Use them beforehand to ensure flow of ink.*

☐ *Plain-sheet notebook. Allows you to mind-map and sketch during ideation stage of negotiation. Rid it of any doodles from previous conversations. Come in clean. (If you've written notes on your negotiation strategy, ensure that they're either coded, abbreviated or illegible.)*

☐ *Business cards.*

☐ *Passport. In case you need to change locations at short notice. Also acts as a back-up to your drivers license should you lose it or have it stolen.*

☐ *Spare cash. Multiple currencies if you work internationally. Don't work up a sweat searching for an ATM at an inconvenient time.*

☐ *Deodorant/cologne. Those negotiation rooms can get hot and sweaty.*

☐ *Toothbrush and toothpaste. You can boost energy mid-negotiation by taking a break to refresh.*

☐ *Medicines. Emergency stash of headache, diarrhea, allergy meds.*

The only thing on the table in front of you should be your notebook and a pen. And your cool, dry hands.

Take this list with you.
Visit bit.ly/Mise_En_Place to download and share.

Hang up the phone. Get on a plane.

Do all you can to avoid negotiating over a phone call. Eye contact is critical. It's entirely worth long train ride or trans-oceanic flight for an hour in the room with an opposing party. So much intent is expressed in non-verbal communication—and trust is built so much more quickly. Language differences that are chasms on the phone can be overcome in a room.

If you absolutely must negotiate on the phone:

Send an agenda ahead of time to provide structure.

If it's a group call, draw a sketch of a table in front of you, mark all the "attendees" of the phone meeting and, using check and gate system, note when everyone speaks. Ensure everyone has a voice, and everyone is heard. A silent participant may feel excluded, hold a grudge—and could later sabotage any constructive agreement.

Words with Friends—and Opponents

Speaking the same language does not we speak the same language. Australians, Americans, Irish, Canadians (many of them), Brits, Kiwis all speak "English". They don't necessarily speak the same language.

"Quite good" in American English means very good. "Quite good" in British English can mean less than good.

(American readers have likely wondered why I keep misspelling words like "practise" or "recognise". Or why the punctuation peskily slips outside quotation marks. British readers will applaud how I got it just right.)

Negotiations are nuanced. Even the most gifted linguists have challenges in understanding nuance in a non-native language. Non-verbal cues are critical. Bottom-line: get in the same room to interpret all the signals.

Traversing the Impasse, Part I

Most negotiations move through one or more moments of seeming impasse, when parties are on the verge of walking away without resolution. Your job is to place a wedge in the frame so the door can't slam shut.

If the tone grows strained, take the parties out of themselves. Provide a release that puts the conversation in perspective.

The William Jefferson Clinton Presidential Library in Little Rock, AR, is a box of glass and steel levitating over the Arkansas River. Outside the to-scale replica of the Oval Office, an interactive video console welcomes visitors to listen to the former President tell a few stories. Including the one about a moon rock.

When parties were days away from historic agreements and iconic Rose Garden handshakes. Before the political breakthroughs, when no one yet knew that a positive outcome was possible. When disagreements were deep, and the voices increasingly ragged with anger and disappointment. President Clinton would hold up his hands. The room would grow quiet. And he'd point at a jagged chunk of white stone resting on the table between them.

It was a moon rock, on loan from NASA, carbon-dated at 3.6 billion years old. It wasn't on the table in the Oval Office by accident. When the air left the room and the negotiation seemed ready to unravel, Clinton would say, "Wait a minute. See that rock? It's 3.6 billion years old. We're all just passing through. Take a deep breath. Calm down. Let's see what makes sense here."

From time to time, we deploy our friend Zoe Romano to speak at dinner during lengthy negotiations. She's an extreme endurance runner—the first human being ever to *run* the Tour de France route. After she's told her tale of running up to 90 miles in a single day, all the parties have context for what is truly "hard". Zoe's role is simple and effective: to contextualise, and encourage endurance.

If you're alert to the environment in which you're negotiating, you'll be able to call upon the resources available to you in the moment of impasse—and use them to help all parties understand their commonalities. You'll open the blinds so all can see the passing of the day: twilight will prompt a desire to reach agreement. You'll note the paintings hanging in the hall. You'll notice who smokes during breaks and who calls their spouse. You'll note who ordered vegetarian food. And you'll call upon your own experiences. Some of these things will be useful. Some won't. But you'll only be able to choose if you're alert.

Traversing the Impasse, Part II

Retreat. Then take another run at it.

Return to the issues on which you aligned. Retrace the points where you overcame disagreement. Regurgitate the previously negotiated items. Then take another run at the sticking point with the wind at your back.

Retrace the points where you overcame disagreement. Then take another run at the sticking point with the wind at your back.

In 1934, a young writer hitchhiked from Minnesota to Key West to knock on Earnest Hemingway's door. He had questions—many of them—and most centered on his quest to be a writer. In an agreeable mood, Hemingway conceded. His advice, captured in an essay for Esquire, included this classic bit:

The best way is always to stop when you are going good and when you know what will happen next. If you do that every day when you are writing a novel you will never be stuck. That is the most valuable thing I can tell you so try to remember it.

The advice is fundamentally about momentum. Knowing where you'll start writing tomorrow, with a scene that is already determined, will kickstart your work. For Hemingway, knowing where to begin in the morning was a kind of psychological trick: a way of persuading yourself that you were moving in the right direction before you'd even begun.

We're insecure people. And we have very short memories. We regularly need affirmation that the endeavor we're engaged in has a good chance of success. Behavioral economists will remind us that we are most attracted to restaurants that are busy. We're more likely to enjoy a film if we've heard close friends describe it positively. And we're more likely to do business with a vendor that once served a competitor.

You can create this kind of influence in the room by aggregating the successes the negotiation or relationship has already achieved.

A Word on "Power"

There's no such thing as absolute power. There are lots of types of power. And each can be reduced or negated by deploying an alternative power. In advance of a negotiation it's worth contemplating the types of power that might be deployed against you, and the options you have to resist, reject or outflank those powers. Here are a few examples I come across often.

REWARD POWER: The ability to deploy rewards, e.g., bonuses, promotions, raises. Your Defence: Do not need it. Keep your core living costs (rent, car payment, etc.) low. Work hard on your Life Mission and Orbit of Matter. We're not advocating for asceticism, and it may sound very Buddhist, but being unmotivated by rewards increases your relative power. If you don't need the carrot, then reward power has little ability to influence you.

INFORMATIONAL POWER: Possessing more information on a subject than another. Defence: Insist as a principle of fair negotiation that all parties have access to the same information.

EXPERT POWER: A party having a deep expertise on a subject or market. Defence: Hire your own temporary expertise. Or agree that an agreement is subject to review by a third-party expert.

CHARISMATIC POWER: A party having the ability to generate high intensity emotional interactions during the negotiation. Defence: Stretch out the negotiations as long as possible. Charisma is hard to maintain for extended periods of time. Go to the bathroom at the same time. It's hard to be under the influence of the charisma of the other while sitting/standing in adjacent stall.[13]

STATUS POWER: Uniforms, titles, grand offices, security details. Don't underestimate how intimidating and distracting these can be. Defence: Host the meeting away from offices, in casual settings. Agree on a standard, equal protocol in advance as to how each will address the other during the negotiations.[14]

[13] I'm serious about this. A reminder that we're all human is a leveler that can balance power.

[14] E.g., "In public we will, of course address Governor Jones as "Governor," but during this negotiation of equals, we'll each be referring to each other by first names, at a venue that is neutral and informal".

INTERPERSONAL POWER: The ability to connect with others, generate empathy and a sense of common tribe. Defence: Limit social time during negotiations, and be careful with the personal details shared during casual moments.

Power comes in innumerable forms, and we'll cover the subject in detail in a future book. For the general purposes of negotiation, simply be sure to reflect on what intimidates you and your team (i.e., What influences you to make sub-optimal agreements?) and be prepared to counteract those vulnerabilities. Don't overthink it. Trust your intuition.

**There's no such thing as absolute power.
There are lots of types of power.
And each can be reduced or negated by
deploying an alternative power.**

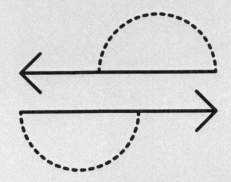

EXECUTION

Negotiation is not about agreement.

It's about faithful execution of agreement.

EXECUTION

Deal Celebrations

Don't host them the day of the deal. Wait until you return home. If your counterparts are watching you lavishly celebrate the deal you've negotiated with them, they may be insulted and question their deal. Be patient. It will feel just as good when you're at a respectful distance.

We recommend delaying celebrations regardless. Celebrate the bedding in of a deal, not the closing of a deal (which is really the true beginning of an agreement).[15]

---

[15] And filing corporate expenses for the lavish party that you celebrated a deal days before it fell apart can look poorly on your career...

No Means No. Yes Means Maybe.

Key to any agreement should be the path to execution. Bed in and commit the parties to the agreement the minute you have the "yes". Hesitation on the execution risks change of mind and reversal of course. Many an able negotiator has let off the gas too early, and watched a tidy agreement spin into disarray.

After yes, move to action. Swiftly. Assign teams for next steps—and detail those steps concisely. Oversee the hand-off to lawyers. Secure key points of agreement in writing.

- ☐ *Assume nothing*
- ☐ *Secure key points of agreement in writing*
- ☐ *Detail next steps concisely*
- ☐ *Assign teams to each of those next steps*
- ☐ *Oversee hand-off to lawyers—whom you have prepped in advance*
- ☐ *Input all observations and learnings into your database for future reference*
- ☐ *Stay ahead of the deal's progress by path-building several steps in advance*
- ☐ *Send personal follow-up communication to key stakeholders—from assistants to executives*

bit.ly/LetsSketch

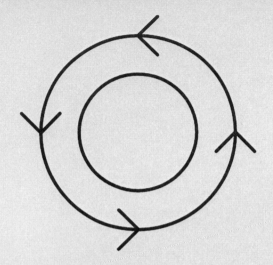

PRACTISE

— THE —

PRACTICE

PRACTISE
— THE —
PRACTICE

Building Muscle

Rehearsal is frequently underutilized. It's time-consuming and requires a commitment of resources, but I've often seen it make the difference between successful and unsuccessful negotiations. Voicing your arguments and counterarguments, getting used to push-back, becoming acquainted with the possible distractions and obstacles—practice rounds surface valuable insights that you'd never have stumbled upon in isolation.

If you can't employ professionals to help you prep for intense negotiations, create as useful an experience as you can by recruiting people with whom you don't necessarily get along very well. Choose people who enjoy proving you wrong—who actually enjoy defeating you. In my office, I know who I want to practise negotiating with, and my closest business friends aren't on the list.

The greatest risk is not that someone who negotiates like you will be a better than you are. Rather, the greatest risk is that someone will be a very different type of negotiator than you, and you'll be unprepared for the encounter. Rehearsal will expose you to different ways of thinking about the subject and the approach.

Negotiation prep is not like football practise. Here, there are no rules. Which means it's all the more important to grow comfortable with the variations, to learn agility, to become familiar with a wide variety of measures. And these are things you only learn with repetition.

In real negotiations all kinds of the unpredictable happen—fire, sickness, drunkenness, tornadoes. You can't prepare for every eventuality, but you can muscularly train yourself to be practiced in flexibly handling any eventuality.

Knowing the Stakes

Few of us, beyond law enforcement officers, crisis health workers and intelligence officers, are typically negotiating immediate life and death issues. But occasionally the muscular training in negotiation techniques falls into place to save oneself considerable pain.

It came down to this: I asked the wrong person for directions.

During the writing of this book, I was visiting in China on business. On the hunt for a particular location in an unfamiliar part of a large city, I stupidly followed a stranger's suggestion to cut through a side street. Three steps into the alley I found myself being mugged at knifepoint by three guys. It's times like these that the practise and training kick in. And by leaning on tools outlined in this book, I was able to negotiate myself out of the situation, relatively unscathed.

At the time, the story seemed fortuitous: a detailed description of the steps I took would make for a dramatic close to this book.

But it's not the right ending. It would place "negotiation" back into the world of Hollywood spies or cops on primetime dramas, when the real value of being a good negotiator reveals itself in *your* day to day. In having millions of people deploy transparent techniques to understand the other party and collaboratively create value for both sides. Save the hostage rescue negotiations for the extreme pros and television dramas. The cartography of negotiation is a creative art for real people.

bit.ly/LetsSketch

APPENDIX

The Negotiator's Diet

Negotiation is demanding work, requiring sustained focus and consistent energy. Which means you'll need your body as much as your mind for the effort.

Zoe Romano is my endurance coach. Not for athletics. For negotiation. An extreme athlete, Zoe's run across the United States, and is the first woman ever to run the course of the Tour de France—that's more than a marathon a day for 50 days. Zoe knows how to prep for the long game.

From my work with Zoe has come The Negotiator's Diet, a simple, prescriptive approach to make sure I'm at my best when I'm needed most. I'm including the basics below.

Most diets proscribe: they denounce certain actions and forbid certain indulgences. Functionally, most diets are a list of what you can't have. We fail so often at dieting because constant resistance requires remarkable emotional energy.

Instead, The Negotiator's Diet is prescriptive, suggesting a list of things you need to do every day. By actively doing these things you fill a void that might otherwise be filled with junk.

Each of these involves active hydration and a slow release of energy that will help you avoid the peaks and slumps produced by sugar and caffeine. This keeps the body alert, the mind aware, and your concentration steady. To endure intense negotiations for protracted periods, this constancy is essential.

The Negotiator's Diet

MORNING

- *20 minutes of active exercise*
- *Oatmeal and Fruit. Top the oatmeal with honey if you like*
- *Decaf coffee. Drink it during the whole day if you wish. Decaf is not caffeine-free, so you'll be getting a steady stream of low-level caffeine*

MID-DAY

- *Lunch: Salad of your choice on a large bed of greens*
- *Afternoon: Fresh fruit, dried fruits, peanuts*

EVENING

- *Happy hour: Ginger ale or ginger beer. Ginger relaxes muscles, reduces inflammation in stomach, soothes sinuses*
- *Dinner: Protein. Lots and lots of vegetables*
- *After-dinner: Decaf espresso*

ALL DAY

- *3 litres of liquid. At least 2 of those should be water*
- *One hour before bed, pick up the newspaper or a book, and switch off all screens, including smart phone, laptop, tablet and television*

Take this list with you.
Visit bit.ly/NegotiatorsDiet to download and share.

The Negotiator's Library

THE BLACK SWAN

Nassim Taleb's brilliant book presents a basic case: we are so bad at predicting the future because we're shaped so heavily by our past. We can't break the frames. While he offers techniques for improving forecasting ability, the core benefit of the book is its encouragement that we surrender the idea that we can know or control the future. Instead: harness what's happening in the current and be part of shaping the future, not just guessing about it.

GETTING TO YES

Roger Fisher and Bill Ury, colleagues at the Harvard Negotiation Project, collaborated on this most classic of negotiation texts. It's a little dry. It's a little old. But it truly shaped the field of negotiation. Fisher has passed away, but Ury is around and very active. Listen to his lectures if you get a chance. And reference their follow-up book Getting Past No.

Your reading library should contain a balance: anchor books you return to frequently matched with a rotating collection of books that provide alternative viewpoints. You can see what I'm reading now by visiting FrontierDispatches.com and tapping Recommended Reading.

PREDICTABLY IRRATIONAL

Dan Ariely's popular book was one of the first to make behavioral economics accessible to those outside research labs. His lively examples and engaging style make the book an enjoyable read, but his critical approach is vital to approaching negotiation realistically: we must understand that logic and rationality are only a small part of the human decision-making process.

THINKING, FAST AND SLOW

Don't think of Daniel Kahneman as a Nobel Prize winner. Though of course he is. Think of him as your negotiation coach, who will constantly remind you with data and anecdote that human judgment is flawed and that bias and illusion are undeniably powerful forces—but ones that can be harnessed if we know how.

THE BLACK BOOK OF COLOR

Practise seeing the world from multiple perspectives. In this case, experiencing colour through the eyes of the blind. A stimulating project from author Menena Cottin and illustrator Rosana Faría.

Take this list with you.
Visit bit.ly/NegotiatorsLibrary to download and share.

Acknowledgments

Most of the experts who generously invested their energies in coaching me in these skills would likely prefer to remain un-named due to potential embarrassment at my mangling of their teachings. So the public thanks go to those at The Frontier Project who have given me the space and provided the inspiration to write this book.

In particular my wife and business partner Ryann Wayne, who has nudged and cajoled me over years into putting fingers to keyboard, and has accepted a life of my disrupting dinners in order to scribble notes on napkins in restaurants across the country.

About the Author

SCOTT WAYNE

Scott Wayne is the Founder of The Frontier Project, one of the fastest-growing private companies in America, and a sought-after speaker and advisor to contemporary leaders. He lives in Richmond, Virginia with his wife and three daughters.

JASON ALLEN ASHLOCK

Jason Allen Ashlock is the Founding Partner of Frontier Press and a Lead Consultant at The Frontier Project.

Visit TheFrontierProject.com and CartographySeries.com to learn more.

About the Series

The everyday practices of good business are as much art as science. Our most difficult and meaningful work—negotiation and innovation, leadership and influence—doesn't fit easily into processes and systems. To succeed at these essentials requires we cultivate the interpretive and creative skills of mapmakers: adaptive to complex landscapes, adept at wayfinding through uncertainty, and alert to all the potential approaches to our final destinations.

Thus: The Cartography Series from FrontierPress. Short books from category experts that translate firsthand research into practical application. If traditional business books are guidebooks for armchair travelers, The Cartography Series is for those brave enough to take the trip. Small enough to fit in a pocket or purse, easily read on a 90-minute flight, and frequently returned to for jolts of insight and instruction. These are the maps to where you're going next.

THE CARTOGRAPHY SERIES

Mapping the Frontier.

The Cartography Series is a product of FrontierPress, the next-generation publishing unit of The Frontier Project. Through innovative publishing initiatives and immersive reading experiences, FrontierPress equips individuals to learn, launch, and lead within their organizations and communities. To learn more, visit FrontierProjectPress.com